D0466598

*Silly things happen each and every day. In the pages just ahead you will meet a pig eating pretzels and a frog with a flat. You'll find Swamp Monsters and a wolf who likes chicken stew. You'll learn about stars in the sky and animals from days gone by. Hold onto your hat and let the laughter begin as we wiggle and giggle our way through another part of*

Illustration from *Fables* by Arnold Lobel.  Copyright © 1980 by Arnold Lobel. Reprinted by permission of Harper & Row, Publishers, Inc. and Jonathan Cape.

Cover Illustration from *Fables* by Arnold Lobel. Copyright © 1980 by
Arnold Lobel. Reprinted by permission of Harper & Row, Publishers, Inc.
and Jonathan Cape.

Acknowledgments appear on page 206.

Copyright © 1991 by Houghton Mifflin Company. All rights reserved.

No part of this work may be reproduced or transmitted in any form or by any
means, electronic or mechanical, including photocopying and recording, or by
any information storage or retrieval system without the prior written permission
of the copyright owner, unless such copying is expressly permitted by federal
copyright law. With the exception of non-profit transcription in Braille,
Houghton Mifflin is not authorized to grant permission for further uses of
copyrighted selections reprinted in this text without the permission of their
owners. Permission must be obtained from the individual copyright owners as
identified herein. Address requests for permission to make copies of Houghton
Mifflin material to School Permissions, Houghton Mifflin Company, One Beacon
Street, Boston, MA 02108.

Printed in the U.S.A.

ISBN: 0-395-51919-5

CDEFGHIJ-VH-9987654321

# Silly Things Happen

Illustration from *Fables* by Arnold Lobel. Copyright © 1980 by Arnold Lobel.
Reprinted by permission of Harper & Row, Publishers, Inc. and Jonathan Cape.

*Senior Author*
John J. Pikulski

*Senior Coordinating Author*
J. David Cooper

*Senior Consulting Author*
William K. Durr

*Coordinating Authors*
Kathryn H. Au
M. Jean Greenlaw
Marjorie Y. Lipson
Susan Page
Sheila W. Valencia
Karen K. Wixson

*Authors*
Rosalinda B. Barrera
Ruth P. Bunyan
Jacqueline L. Chaparro
Jacqueline C. Comas
Alan N. Crawford
Robert L. Hillerich
Timothy G. Johnson
Jana M. Mason
Pamela A. Mason
William E. Nagy
Joseph S. Renzulli
Alfredo Schifini

*Senior Advisor*
Richard C. Anderson

*Advisors*
Christopher J. Baker
Charles Peters

HOUGHTON MIFFLIN COMPANY   BOSTON
Atlanta   Dallas   Geneva, Illinois   Palo Alto   Princeton   Toronto

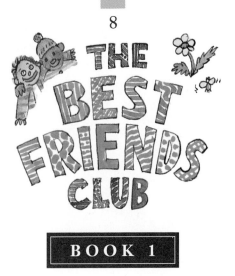

## THE BEST FRIENDS CLUB

**BOOK 1**

12  Lizzie and Harold  *by Elizabeth Winthrop*

32  Ira Says Goodbye  *by Bernard Waber*

58  Gloria Who Might Be My Best Friend
*from* The Stories Julian Tells
*by Ann Cameron*

POETRY
30  What Johnny Told Me
*by John Ciardi*
Two Friends  *by Nikki Giovanni*
31  Since Hanna Moved Away
*by Judith Viorst*

THEME BOOK
Henry and Mudge
*by Cynthia Rylant*

# FUNNY BUSINESS

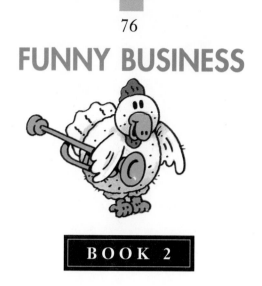

**BOOK 2**

80  The Wolf's Chicken Stew  *by Keiko Kasza*

92  Swamp Monsters  *by Mary Blount Christian*

114  Amelia Bedelia  *by Peggy Parish*

POETRY
107  What Did?  *by Shel Silverstein*
108  The Folk Who Live in Backward Town
*by Mary Ann Hoberman*
109  A Puppy  *by Oliver Herford*
110  Eletelephony  *by Laura E. Richards*
111  Bananananananananana  *by William Cole*
112  At the Beach  *by John Ciardi*
113  There Was a Sad Pig with a Tail  *by Arnold Lobel*
Bursting  *by Dorothy Aldis*

📖

THEME BOOK
Monkey-Monkey's Trick
*by Patricia McKissack*

132

# THE WORLD OF INFORMATION

**BOOK 3**

136  Do You Know About Stars?
*by Mae Blacker Freeman*

156  Dinosaur Time  *by Peggy Parish*

180  Air Is All Around You
*by Franklyn M. Branley*

THEME BOOK
The Biggest, Smallest, Fastest,
Tallest Things You've Ever Heard Of
*by Robert Lopshire*

GLOSSARY
198

BOOK 1

THE
BEST
FRIENDS
CLUB

# WELCOME to the BEST FRIENDS CLUB

Here you'll meet Lizzie and Harold, Ira and Reggie, and Julian and Gloria. They're already friends with each other, and now they're waiting inside to become your friends.

Club Rules:

1. Friends stay friends even if one moves away.
2. Best friends share with one another.
3. Anyone can be a best friend.

10

# Contents

**Lizzie and Harold**  **12**
by *Elizabeth Winthrop*

**Ira Says Goodbye**  **32**
*written and illustrated*
*by Bernard Waber*

**Gloria Who Might Be**
**My Best Friend**  **58**
*from* The Stories
Julian Tells
by *Ann Cameron*

11

# Lizzie and Harold

*by Elizabeth Winthrop*

*illustrated by Martha Weston*

**M**ore than anything else, Lizzie wanted a best friend.

"How do you get a best friend?" she asked her mother.

"You don't really *get* a best friend," her mother answered. "Usually they just happen if you wait."

But Lizzie did not
want to wait. She wanted
a best friend right away.

"Today I am going to find my best friend," Lizzie told Harold.

Harold lived next door. Every day they walked to school together.

"Why do you want a best friend?" Harold asked.

"Because I need someone to tell secrets to and I want someone to teach me cat's cradle and I want someone who likes me as much as I like her," Lizzie said.

"I'll be your best friend," Harold said.

"You can't be," Lizzie said. "You're a boy."

"So what?" said Harold.

But Lizzie did not answer.

The next day Lizzie wore a pink flowered dress and black party shoes to school. Her hair was tied in two ponytails with pink ribbons.

"You look funny," Harold said.

"I look like Christina," Lizzie answered. "She is going to be my new best friend."

"I like you best when you look like Lizzie," Harold said.

When Lizzie got
to school, she ran
up to Christina.

"Hello," said Lizzie.
"I'm wearing my hair just like yours."

Christina did not answer.

"I'm wearing a dress and party shoes just like you,"
said Lizzie. "I brought a piece of string so you could
teach me cat's cradle. I want you to be my best friend."

"I don't want a best friend," Christina said.

"You don't?" said Lizzie.

"No," said Christina.

She walked away.

"How's your new friend?" Harold
asked on the way home.

"Don't ask," said Lizzie. "Christina's
not my best friend after all."

"That was quick," said Harold.

"I have a new idea," Lizzie said.

"What is it?" Harold asked.

"You'll see," said Lizzie.

The next day, Lizzie put a sign on the
front door of her house.
    The doorbell rang.  Lizzie ran to open it.

There stood Harold.

"Here I am," he said. "Your new best friend."

"You can't be my best friend," Lizzie said. "You're a boy, and you're only five and three quarters."

"I learned how to do cat's cradle," Harold said.

"You did?" Lizzie said. "Can you teach it to me?"

"Sure," Harold said.

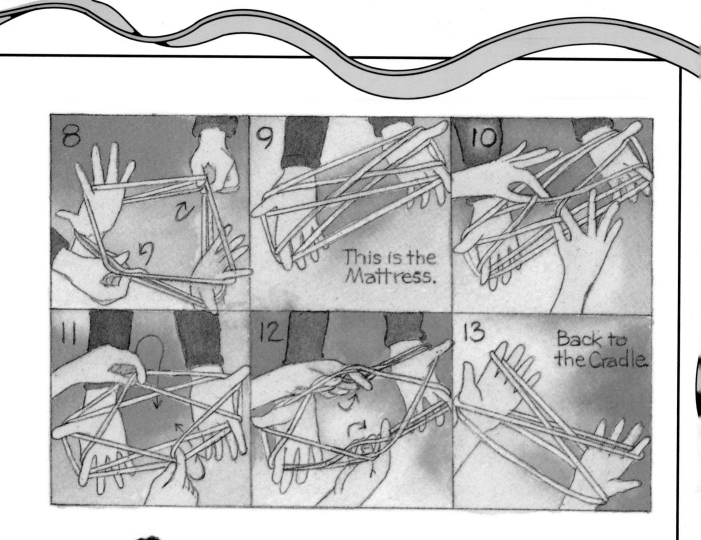

"I'll teach you Jacob's Ladder and Teacup and
Saucer and Witch's Hat tomorrow," Harold said.

Nobody else rang the doorbell.
Lizzie took down the sign.
"Does that mean I'm your best
friend now?" Harold asked.
"No," said Lizzie. "That means
I give up. I don't want a best friend
after all."

The next day Harold was carrying a big
blue bag to school.
"What's in your bag?" asked Lizzie.
"It's my trick-or-treat candy," said Harold.

"Why are you taking it to school?" asked Lizzie.

"I'm going to give it to the person who promises to be my best friend," said Harold. "Since you don't want to be my best friend, I'm going to find somebody else."

"Harold, you can't find a best friend that way," Lizzie said.

"Why not?" asked Harold.

"Because best friends just happen to you. You can't go out and buy them. Besides, I thought you wanted to be *my* best friend," Lizzie cried.

But Harold wasn't listening.

All day long Lizzie thought about Harold. When she met him after school, he did not have his blue bag of candy.

"I have a new best friend," Harold said. "He is a boy. He is five and a half years old. He ate all my candy and his name is Douglas."

"Why do you look so sad?" Lizzie asked.

"Because I like you better," said Harold.

"Well, I have a new best friend too," Lizzie said.
"He is a boy.  He is five and three quarters years old.
He knows how to do cat's cradle and he likes me as
much as I like him."

Harold looked even sadder.

"What's his name?" Harold asked.

"Harold," said Lizzie.

# Cat's Cradle

Friends share what they know with each other. In the story, Harold taught Lizzie how to play cat's cradle. You could show one of your friends how to play cat's cradle. All you need is a piece of string and the pictures in the story. Practice the steps until you are sure you understand them. Then explain them to a friend.

## What Johnny Told Me

I went to play with Billy. He
Threw my cap into a tree.
I threw his glasses in the ditch.
He dipped my shirt in a bucket of pitch.
I hid his shoes in the garbage can.
And then we heard the ice cream man.
So I bought him a cone. He bought
me one.
A true good friend is a lot of fun!

John Ciardi

## Two Friends

lydia and shirley have
two pierced ears and
two bare ones
five pigtails
two pairs of sneakers
two berets
two smiles
one necklace
one bracelet
lots of stripes and
one good friendship

Nikki Giovanni

# Since Hanna Moved Away

The tires on my bike are flat.
The sky is grouchy gray.
At least it sure feels like that
Since Hanna moved away.

Chocolate ice cream tastes like prunes.
December's come to stay.
They've taken back the Mays and Junes
Since Hanna moved away.

Flowers smell like halibut.
Velvet feels like hay.
Every handsome dog's a mutt
Since Hanna moved away.

Nothing's fun to laugh about.
Nothing's fun to play.
They call me, but I won't come out
Since Hanna moved away.

Judith Viorst

# IRA SAYS GOODBYE

*written and illustrated by Bernard Waber*

Reggie, my best friend, was moving away. My sister was the first to tell me about it.

This is how she told me. She said: "I . . . ra . . . !"

"What?" I said.

"Do I have a surprise for you!"

(I knew, right away, I would hate the surprise.)

"What?" I said.

"What I just heard."

(I knew, right away, I shouldn't say *what* again.)

"What?" I said again.

"Guess," she said.

"GOODBYE!" I said.

"Wait!" she said.

"Somebody is going to be doing something."

"What?" I said.

"Real soon."

"What?" I said.

"Something."

"GOODBYE!" I said.

"Wait!" she said.

"Moving," she said.

"Somebody is moving?" I said.

"In two weeks."

"Who?" I said.

"Aren't you going to guess?"

"Whoooooooooooo?" I said.

"Not even one little, teenie, tiny guess?"

"GOODBYE!" I said.

"Wait!" she said.
"Reggie!"
"What!" I said.
"Your best friend."
"Is moving?"
"Away," she said. "Far, far away.
Oh, I would hate it to pieces if my best
friend were moving away. What will you do
when your best friend in the whole wide world
moves away? Hmmmmm?"

"I don't believe it," I said.
"Believe it," she said.

I ran into the house.

"It's true," said my mother.

"We were just coming to tell you," said my father.

"We learned about it only minutes ago," said my mother.

"But it's not as though you won't ever see Reggie again," said my father. "Greendale is only an hour's drive."

"Greendale?" I said.

"Where Reggie will be living," said my mother.

"And you can always talk on the telephone," said my father.

"But talking on the telephone won't be the same," I said.

"I know," said my mother.

"I know," said my father.

Reggie, moving! I couldn't
believe it. Reggie was my best friend
as far back as I could remember.

We had our own tree house and
a secret hiding place that only we
knew about because it was so secret.

And we had a magic act: the Amazing Reggie and the Fantastic Ira. Everyone came to see us perform.

And we had our own club: The Dolphins. So far, there were only two members — us. But we thought it was a good start.

I went to all of Reggie's birthday parties. And he came to all of mine.

We put our baseball cards together, so that way it would make a bigger pile.

When Reggie was away on vacation, I took care of his dog, Herman. He did the same for Geraldine, my cat.

And when Reggie was sick in the hospital, I sent him a get-well card. I made it myself.

And when I was away, visiting my grandparents in Oregon, Reggie sent me a miss-you card.

We even put our turtles together in the same tank,
so they could be best friends too — like us. My turtle
was Felix. His was Oscar.

I decided to go and find
Reggie, and tell him how
sorry I felt to hear he was
moving away.

I found Reggie.
We both started talking
at the same time.
    "You're moving," I said.
    "We're moving," he said.
    "To Greendale," I said.
    "To Greendale," he said.
    And then he said, "My
father has a new job."

    "In Greendale," I said.
    Reggie sighed.  I sighed too.
    "We can still talk on the telephone," I said.
    "But that won't be the same," said Reggie.
    "I know," I said.

But the next day, to my surprise, Reggie wasn't the same Reggie anymore.

"Isn't it terrible?" I said.

"Isn't it terrific?" he said.

I looked at Reggie. "Did you just say terrific?"

"Uh-huh," said Reggie.

"Did you just say uh-huh?" I said.

"Uh-huh," said Reggie.

I couldn't believe it. I said to Reggie, "When you just said uh-huh, the way you just said uh-huh, did you mean — uh-huh — you're glad you're moving?"

"Uh-huh," said Reggie.

Reggie started to explain: "Greendale is going to be so great," he said. "Great, great, great! My father told me all about it — last night. In Greendale, all people do is have fun. Fun, fun, fun, all of the time. Listen to this: There's this place in Greendale where they keep this killer shark. Every day, people go to this place to see this killer shark — just so they can get scared. Because the minute this killer shark sees everybody, he starts to snort."

"Sharks snort?" I said.

"This one snorts," said Reggie. "And he makes killer shark faces at everybody, because that's what killer sharks love best to do, make ugly, scary killer shark faces at people. Isn't that great!"

"And do you know what else about Greendale?" said Reggie. "There's this park, with games and thriller rides. And all people do all day, in Greendale, is play these games, and scream their heads off riding these thriller rides — and watch fireworks Saturday nights. Isn't that great!"

"And do you know what else about Greendale?" said Reggie. "There's this lake, with swans and ducks, and cute little baby swans and ducks too. And the minute these swans and ducks see you coming, they just scoot right up to you, just so you can feed them. Isn't that great!"

"And the people in Greendale are so friendly," said Reggie. "All they do, all day long, is go around smiling. Smiling, smiling, smiling, all of the time. They just never get tired of smiling. And they give you this big hello, no matter how many times they see you. Even if they see you two hundred times a day, they'll stop and say hello. Isn't that great!"

"People here are friendly," I said. "Some are even best friends."

But Reggie just went on talking about Greendale, as if he had never heard about best friends.

"Oh, I almost forgot the most terrific part," said Reggie, "the part about my Uncle Steve. He plays football for the Greendale Tigers, you know. And I'll be seeing him every day. And he's going to teach me to kick and pass, so that when I grow up, I'll play football for the Greendale Tigers too. Isn't that great!"

Reggie looked at me. "Isn't that great!" he said again.

"Uh-huh," I said.

Day after day, Reggie had new stories to tell about Greendale. He never seemed to want to do any of our old things anymore, like going up to the tree house or performing the magic act. He even took back his top hat, cape, and wand, which were kept at the secret hiding place. And while he was at it, he took his baseball cards. It was as if Reggie had already moved away.

One day, Reggie came by to take back Oscar, his turtle. It was my turn to keep the tank.

"But Felix and Oscar are friends," I said. "They're used to being together."

"They're only turtles," said Reggie.

"Turtles have feelings," I said. "And nobody can explain to a turtle why his friend isn't with him anymore."

"Nothing bothers turtles," said Reggie.

"Turtles are bothered. They're bothered a whole lot," I said. "Turtles get lonely. And they get sad — especially if a friend is taken away. And they start to mope."

"Turtles do not mope," said Reggie.

"They do so mope," I said. "Everybody knows that. And they stop eating. And they get sick — even die. Do you want that to happen, Reggie?"

"They don't die," said Reggie, "not from losing a friend."

"They do, too, die," I said. "Everybody knows that about turtles. Everybody who isn't stupid knows that."

"I'm taking Oscar," said Reggie.

"Then take Felix, too," I said.

Reggie looked at me. "Do you mean it?" he said.

"Uh-huh," I said.

And that's just what happened. Reggie walked out with Oscar — and Felix.

Maybe I shouldn't have said that part about being stupid. But sometimes Reggie gets to me. Sometimes Reggie really gets to me. Like whenever I call Reggie on the telephone, and I say to him, "What are you doing?" He always says, "Talking to you" — like I didn't know he was talking to me. I can't tell you how many times he pulled that one.

Do you want to know something else about Reggie? When Reggie eats lunch, he always laughs with his mouth wide open, and with all that yuckie food showing. I hate that about Reggie.

And Reggie doesn't care one bit about friends. He really doesn't. He didn't care one bit how lonely Felix and Oscar would feel without each other.

Do you want to know something? I just hope some new kid moves into Reggie's old house; some new kid who will be my best friend; some new kid who won't always be bragging about his uncle the football player.

Do you want to know something else? I can't wait for Reggie to move.

Do you want to know something else? I will jump for joy the day Reggie moves away.

I didn't have to wait long. One day, a big van pulled up to Reggie's house. I watched as the men carried everything out of the house.

When the house was empty, Reggie and his parents came outside.

Reggie was carrying the tank with Felix and Oscar in it. My parents and sister were there too. Everyone hugged and said goodbye — everyone except Reggie and me.

"Aren't you two going to say goodbye?" said Reggie's mother.

Suddenly, Reggie burst out crying and couldn't stop. He cried and cried, and no amount of patting seemed to help.

"Reggie is taking this move so hard," said his father.

At last, when Reggie stopped crying, he handed me the tank. He said, "Here, Ira, you keep them."

"You're giving Felix and Oscar to me?" I said.

"Uh-huh," said Reggie.

I was so surprised.

I dug into my pocket for my baseball cards, and handed Reggie the one I always knew he wanted.

"You're giving me your favorite card!" said Reggie.

"Uh-huh," I said.

This time it was Reggie's turn to be surprised.

We all waved goodbye as Reggie and his parents drove away. When their car disappeared, we looked at each other. Everyone was sad.

"There's only one thing to do at a time like this," said my mother.

"What?" I said.

"Let's go into the house and bake a cake."

"Excellent," said my father.

"What kind of cake?" said my sister.

"How about angel food?" said my mother.

And that's just what we did, the day Reggie moved.

We baked a cake.

That night,
the telephone
rang. "It's for
you, Ira," said
my father.

It was Reggie.
"What are you doing?" he said.
"Talking to you," I said.

"Stop fooling," said Reggie.

"I'm eating cake," I said.

"Listen," said Reggie, "would you like
to visit at my house this weekend? My
father and I can pick you up."

"Oh, would I!" I said. "Will your
uncle Steve be there?"

"Uh-huh," said Reggie.

"Great!" I said.
"I can't wait."

"Just a minute,"
said Reggie. "My
mother wants to ask
your mother if it's all
right for you to come."

My mother got on the telephone.
"Say yes," I whispered.
"Yes . . . I mean . . . hello!
Oh, hello, Ellie!"
Ellie is Reggie's mother.
"How are things?" said my mother.
"Say yes," I whispered.
My mother said, "Uh-huh."
And then she said some more "uh-huhs."
And then she said, "Yes.  Yes, yes, yes,"
she kept saying.

Yes, yes, yes, I kept shaking my head.
And then she said, "Oh, won't that
be nice!"
I knew what she meant by "nice."
"It will be very nice," I whispered.
"You're sure it won't be trouble?"
she said.
"It won't be trouble," I shook my head.
"Saturday." My mother looked at me
hugging myself. "I know he'll be
delighted," she said.

My mother hung up. "Guess what?" she said.

"I'm invited to Reggie's house," I called out, as I ran up the stairs.

"Ira, where are you rushing to?" said my father.

"Up to pack," I said.

"But you're not leaving until Saturday," said my mother. "You have two whole days to pack."

"I don't want to be late," I said.

# It Happened to Me

Even best friends can have problems. Ira had a problem because his best friend was moving away. Write a few sentences about a problem that you and one of your friends have had. Be sure to tell how you solved it.

from
**The Stories
Julian Tells**

# *Gloria*

# *Who Might Be My Best Friend*

*by Ann Cameron*

*illustrated by Beth Peck*

If you have a girl for a friend, people find
out and tease you. That's why I didn't want a
girl for a friend — not until this summer,
when I met Gloria.

It happened one afternoon when I was walking down the street by myself. My mother was visiting a friend of hers, and Huey was visiting a friend of his. Huey's friend is five and so I think he is too young to play with. And there aren't any kids just my age. I was walking down the street feeling lonely.

A block from our house I saw a moving van in front of a brown house, and men were carrying in chairs and tables and bookcases and boxes full of I don't know what. I watched for a while, and suddenly I heard a voice right behind me.

"Who are you?"

I turned around and there was a girl in a yellow dress. She looked the same age as me. She had curly hair that was braided into two pigtails with red ribbons at the ends.

"I'm Julian," I said. "Who are you?"

"I'm Gloria," she said. "I come from Newport. Do you know where Newport is?"

I wasn't sure, but I didn't tell Gloria. "It's a town on the ocean," I said.

"Right," Gloria said. "Can you turn a cartwheel?"

She turned sideways herself and did two cartwheels on the grass.

I had never tried a cartwheel before, but I tried to copy Gloria. My hands went down in the grass, my feet went up in the air, and — I fell over.

I looked at Gloria to see if she was laughing at me. If she was laughing at me, I was going to go home and forget about her.

But she just looked at me very seriously and said, "It takes practice," and then I liked her.

"I know where there's a bird's nest in your yard," I said.

"Really?" Gloria said. "There weren't any trees in the yard, or any birds, where I lived before."

I showed her where a robin lives and has eggs. Gloria stood up on a branch and looked in. The eggs were small and pale blue. The mother robin squawked at us, and she and the father robin flew around our heads.

"They want us to go away," Gloria said. She got down from the branch, and we went around to the front of the house and watched the moving men carry two rugs and a mirror inside.

"Would you like to come over to my house?" I said.

"All right," Gloria said, "if it is all right with my mother." She ran in the house and asked.

It was all right, so Gloria and I went to my house, and I showed her my room and my games and my rock collection, and then I made strawberry punch and we sat at the kitchen table and drank it.

"You have a red mustache on your mouth," Gloria said.

"You have a red mustache on your mouth, too," I said.

Gloria giggled, and we licked off the mustaches with our tongues.

"I wish you'd live here a long time," I told Gloria.

Gloria said, "I wish I would too.

"I know the best way to make wishes," Gloria said.

"What's that?" I asked.

"First you make a kite. Do you know how to make one?"

"Yes," I said, "I know how." I know how to make good kites because my father taught me. We make them out of two crossed sticks and folded newspaper.

"All right," Gloria said, "that's the first part of making wishes that come true. So let's make a kite."

We went out into the garage and spread out sticks and newspaper and made a kite. I fastened on the kite string and went to the closet and got rags for the tail.

"Do you have some paper and two pencils?" Gloria asked. "Because now we make the wishes."

I didn't know what she was planning, but I went in the house and got pencils and paper.

"All right," Gloria said. "Every wish you want to have come true you write on a long thin piece of paper. You don't tell me your wishes, and I don't tell you mine. If you tell, your wishes don't come true. Also, if you look at the other person's wishes, your wishes don't come true."

Gloria sat down on the garage floor and started writing her wishes. I wanted to see what they were — but I went to the other side of the garage and wrote my own wishes instead. I wrote:

1. I wish I could see the catalog cats.

2. I wish the fig tree would be the tallest in town.

3. I wish I'd be a great soccer player.

4. I wish I could ride in an airplane.

5. I wish Gloria would stay here and be my best friend.

I folded my five wishes in my fist and went over to Gloria.

"How many wishes did you make?" Gloria asked.

"Five," I said. "How many did you make?"

"Two," Gloria said.

I wondered what they were.

"Now we put the wishes on the tail of the kite," Gloria said. "Every time we tie one piece of rag on the tail, we fasten a wish in the knot. You can put yours in first."

I fastened mine in, and then Gloria fastened in hers, and we carried the kite into the yard.

"You hold the tail," I told Gloria, "and I'll pull."

We ran through the back yard with the kite, passed the garden and the fig tree, and went into the open field beyond our yard.

The kite started to rise. The tail jerked heavily like a long white snake. In a minute the kite passed the roof of my house and was climbing toward the sun.

We stood in the open field, looking up at it. I was wishing I would get my wishes.

"I know it's going to work!" Gloria said.

"How do you know?"

"When we take the kite down," Gloria told me, "there shouldn't be one wish in the tail. When the wind takes all your wishes, that's when you know it's going to work."

The kite stayed up for a long time. We both held the string. The kite looked like a tiny black spot in the sun, and my neck got stiff from looking at it.

"Shall we pull it in?" I asked.

"All right," Gloria said.

We drew the string in more and more until, like a tired bird, the kite fell at our feet.

We looked at the tail. All our wishes were gone. Probably they were still flying higher and higher in the wind.

Maybe I would see the catalog cats and get to be a good soccer player and have a ride in an airplane and the tallest fig tree in town. And Gloria would be my best friend.

"Gloria," I said, "did you wish we would be friends?"

"You're not supposed to ask me that!" Gloria said.

"I'm sorry," I answered. But inside I was smiling. I guessed one thing Gloria wished for. I was pretty sure we would be friends.

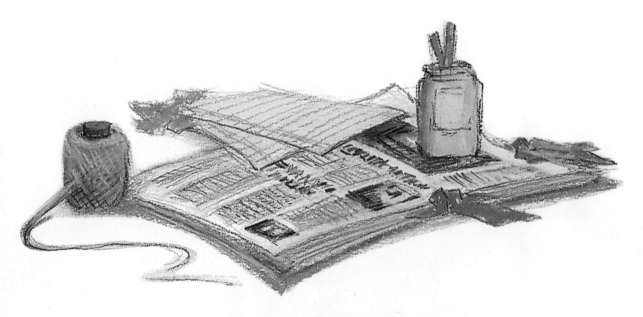

DON'T TELL YOUR WISHES,
WHATEVER YOU DO.
THEN MAYBE YOUR WISHES
WILL ALL COME TRUE!

MY WISH KITE

Make a wish kite
with one of your friends.
Here are the things
you will need:
- a large piece of colored paper
- six small pieces of paper
- tape, scissors
- a long piece of string
- a pencil and crayons

First draw a kite on the large piece of paper. Then cut out the kite. Next, tape a piece of string on for the tail. Then you and your friend should each write three wishes on the small pieces of paper. Finally, tape your wishes onto the tail of the kite.

71

Elizabeth Winthrop has written many stories for children. Some of her stories are serious, and some are very funny. She wrote her first book when she was only twelve years old.

You can read more about Lizzie and Harold in the book *Best Friends Club*. In this book, Lizzie and Harold learn that three friends can be even better than two.

Bernard Waber began writing children's books when his own children were growing up. After Waber wrote stories about Lyle the Crocodile, his friends gave him presents shaped like crocodiles. Soon his house was full of all kinds of crocodiles!

You may enjoy reading these books by Waber.

- **An Anteater Named Arthur**
  Sometimes Arthur is messy and forgetful. Most of the time, his mother thinks he's wonderful.

- **Ira Sleeps Over**
  Reggie invites Ira to spend the night. This story takes place before *Ira Says Goodbye*.

Ann Cameron had a friend named Julian who told her many funny stories about his childhood. Her friend's funny stories gave Cameron the idea of writing a book about growing up.

You might like to read more about Julian in these books.

- **More Stories Julian Tells**
  What do catalog cats, fig trees, and lemon pudding have in common? Julian will tell you.

- **Julian's Glorious Summer**
  Gloria has a new bike, but Julian doesn't like bikes. Gloria has all summer to change his mind.

# More Clubhouse Reading

## Henry and Mudge

*by Cynthia Rylant*

Henry and his dog, Mudge,
are the best of friends and
do everything together.

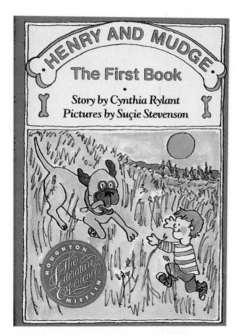

## Best Friends for Frances

*by Russell Hoban*

What will Frances do when her best
friend Albert starts to play boys-only
games?

**The Hating Book** *by Charlotte Zolotow*
How could two such good friends be so mad
at each other?

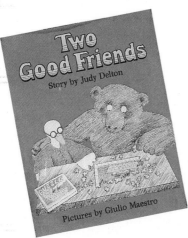

**Two Good Friends** *by Judy Delton*
Bear is messy. Duck is neat. Two friends
learn to share what each one does best.

**Nice New Neighbors** *by Franz Brandenberg*
Everybody seems too busy to make friends
with the new children in the neighborhood.

TO FIND OUT THE ANSWERS TO THESE THREE RIDDLES, READ *FUNNY BUSINESS!*

# TABLE OF CONTENTS

**The Wolf's Chicken Stew**　　80
written and illustrated
by Keiko Kasza

**Swamp Monsters**　　92
by Mary Blount Christian
with illustrations
by Marc Brown

**Amelia Bedelia**　　114
by Peggy Parish
with illustrations
by Fritz Siebel

# The Wolf's Chicken Stew

## Keiko Kasza

There once lived a wolf who loved to eat more than anything else in the world. As soon as he finished one meal, he began to think of the next.

One day the wolf got
a terrible craving for
chicken stew.

All day long he
walked across the forest in
search of a delicious chicken.
Finally he spotted one.

"Ah, she is just perfect for my
stew," he thought.

The wolf crept closer.  But
just as he was about to grab his
prey . . . he had another idea.

"If there were just some way to
fatten this bird a little more," he
thought, "there would be all the
more stew for me."

So . . . the wolf ran
home to his kitchen, and
he began to cook.

84

First he made a hundred scrumptious pancakes. Then, late at night, he left them on the chicken's porch.

"Eat well, my pretty chicken," he cried. "Get nice and fat for my stew!"

The next night he brought a hundred scrumptious doughnuts.

"Eat well, my pretty chicken," he cried. "Get nice and fat for my stew!"

And on the next night he brought a scrumptious cake weighing a hundred pounds.

"Eat well, my pretty chicken," he cried. "Get nice and fat for my stew!"

At last, all was ready.
This was the night he had
been waiting for. He put
a large stew pot on the
fire and set out joyfully to
find his dinner.

"That chicken must be as fat as a balloon by now," he thought. "Let's see."

But as he peeked into the chicken's house . . . the door opened suddenly and the chicken screeched, "Oh, so it was you, Mr. Wolf!"

"Children, children! Look, the pancakes and the doughnuts and that scrumptious cake — they weren't from Santa Claus! All those presents were from Uncle Wolf!"

The baby chicks jumped all over the wolf and gave him a hundred kisses.

"Oh, thank you, Uncle Wolf! You're the best cook in the world!"

Uncle Wolf didn't have chicken stew that night but Mrs. Chicken fixed him a nice dinner anyway.

"Aw, shucks," he thought, as he walked home, "maybe tomorrow I'll bake the little critters a hundred scrumptious cookies!"

# "OH, THANK YOU, UNCLE WOLF!"

Uncle Wolf says that he may bake a hundred scrumptious cookies for the baby chicks. If he does, the chicks will certainly want to thank him. Write a thank-you song for the chicks to sing to Uncle Wolf. Use a tune you already know, like "Twinkle, Twinkle, Little Star," "Happy Birthday," or "Who's Afraid of the Big Bad Wolf?" Then, if you want, sing your song to your classmates.

# SWAMP MONSTERS

Mary Blount Christian
pictures by Marc Brown

Crag pulled the tadpole by the tail. It swam away behind some weeds.

"Stop teasing the tadpoles," Mrs. Swamp Monster said. "And come eat your lunch."

Crag made a face.

"Snail stew, kelp salad," he whined. "Why can't we eat *good* things?"

"Yeah," Fenny said. "Like ice cream or pizza!"

He gave Spot a piece of snail. Spot gobbled it up.

"Don't feed the 'gator at the table," Mrs. Monster said. "It teaches him bad manners. You know we swamp monsters don't eat ice cream and pizza. Those are *people* foods, like in the books we read."

Crag pulled Spot's tail. The 'gator let out a loud *gronk*!

"That's it!" Mrs. Monster said. "Sometimes you both act as bad as — as CHILDREN! Go and play," she said.

"Let's play Children," Crag said.

"Okay," Fenny said. "That's a good game. But we have to dress up first."

They dug through their toy boxes. They found hats and rubber boots to wear. They found the people masks  they wore last Halloween. They crawled out into the swamp.

"*RRRRRRRRroarrr,*" Crag said. "I am a child. I am going to catch you!"

"Shh!" Fenny said. "I hear noises over there."

They peeked through the bushes.

"What are *those*?" Crag asked.

"Don't touch that, Herbie!" the tall one yelled. "That's poison ivy!"

"Is that a people?" Crag asked.

"She looks like the big one in our storybook," Fenny agreed. "But I didn't think they were *real*!"

"Cindy, get back in line! You'll get lost! Jason, don't put rocks in your ears," the tall one yelled.

The tall one talked to herself.

"Oh, *why* did I take Mrs. Smith's class today? I hope she is well soon."

"Children!" she called. "Get in line! It's time to go!"

94

"Did you hear that?" Crag asked Fenny. "She called the short ones children."

Fenny nodded. "I would like to see one REAL close," he said.

They moved closer. Suddenly the tall one grabbed them.

"You heard me!" she said. "Get in line right now. March!"

"Ms. Mumfrey," a girl whined. "Tommy put a bug in my hair."

"Which one is Tommy?" the tall one asked.

"She hit me," a boy said.

Ms. Mumfrey pulled them apart.

"But Mrs. Smith lets us play like this," the boy said.

"Well, Mrs. Smith is sick. You must be extra good for me."

"Listen," Crag said. "She is not their real teacher. And she thinks we are with them."

"Let's go with them," Fenny said. "We can see if the books are true."

Ms. Mumfrey marched them to a big yellow bus. Crag and Fenny got on the bus too. The door shut. The bus bumped and rumbled down the road. Soon the swamp was out of sight. The bus stopped.

"Everyone out!" Ms. Mumfrey said.

The children punched and pushed on the way out.
Crag and Fenny stumbled out too.

"Take off your coats," Ms. Mumfrey said.

"Look!" Fenny said. "The children took off their
skins. They hung them up!"

"You too," Ms. Mumfrey told them.

She pulled and tugged at them.

"Your zippers must be stuck," she said.

The children sat at their desks.

"Take your seats," Ms. Mumfrey told Crag and Fenny.

Crag asked Fenny, "Where should we take them?"

"I don't know," Fenny said. "But we don't want to make her mad."

They picked up their chairs and carried them toward the door. The children laughed.

"I like the new kids," Tommy said.

"Stop that!" Ms. Mumfrey said. "You would not do this to Mrs. Smith!"

She hit the desk with a ruler.

"Sit down in the seats," she said. "It's time for our TV art lesson. You there," she told Crag. "Put on the TV."

Crag saw the box in the corner. It was like the one in his storybook. But he did not know how to put it on. He didn't want her mad at him though. He thought it might fit on his head. So that is where he put it.

"Stop that!" Ms. Mumfrey yelled.

"The new kids are neat!" Marshall said.

Ms. Mumfrey put the TV on the table. She turned the knob. A picture came on.

"Today we will finger-paint," it said.

Ms. Mumfrey smiled.

"Yes, we will finger-paint," she said.

The children got paints and paper. Crag and Fenny found some too. The children swooshed paint on the paper.

"That looks like *paper* painting to me," Crag said. "But Ms. Mumfrey said to *finger*-paint."

"We don't want to make her mad," Fenny said.

They painted their fingers. It felt good. They took off their boots and painted their toes. The children giggled. They all painted their fingers and toes too.

Ms. Mumfrey held her head.

"Why me?" she moaned. "It is lunchtime. Come here if you need lunch money."

Crag and Fenny didn't have anything like that. They went to her desk. Ms. Mumfrey put a quarter, a dime, and a nickel into Crag's hand.

"But I wanted ice cream," he told Fenny.

"Don't make her mad," Fenny said.

So Crag popped the money into his mouth. Ms. Mumfrey gasped. Crag swallowed. The money clinked into his tummy.

"Never do I want another day like this!" Ms. Mumfrey said.

She gave Crag more money.

"Don't eat this," she said. "This is for the lunchroom."

The lunchroom was not to eat either. That was where they lined up to push and shove each other.

"Oh, boy!" Marshall said. "Noodles and ice cream."

Crag and Fenny were glad they could eat their storybook foods. Crag looked at the noodles.

"They look like worms," he said.

"The ice cream looks like snow," Fenny said.

"Maybe it tastes better than it looks," Crag said.

"Take your seats," Ms. Mumfrey said. "I mean, SIT DOWN!" she said.

Crag chased the noodles all around his plate. They wiggled away. He stabbed some with his fork. He got them almost to his mouth. They flopped back to the plate.

Fenny tried to eat the ice cream. It dripped all over him. It felt sticky and cold.

"I wish I had snail stew," Fenny said.

After that they went outside.

"Now, go play," Ms. Mumfrey said.

"Look," Crag said. "Those children hit that big white berry with a stick. And those are swinging from a metal tree."

Then they saw it. "It is like the swamp!" Crag said.

They both jumped into the fountain. They splashed lovely wet water on themselves. The other children jumped in too.

"Eeeeek!" Ms. Mumfrey yelled. "You act like — like MONSTERS!"

She wagged her finger at them. "The principal will straighten you out!"

"That would hurt," Crag said.

"I like being round," Fenny agreed.

They got out of the water. Ms. Mumfrey dried them off. They went inside.

"It is story time," she said. "Put your heads on your desks."

Crag and Fenny were glad that she didn't really mean it. She only wanted them to rest their heads on the desks.

"She sure talks funny," Crag said.

"Far, far away in a warm, wet swamp," Ms. Mumfrey read, "lived some monsters."

Crag peeked at Fenny. He looked sad too.

"They ate snails and fish and turtle eggs," she read.

Crag's tummy rumbled. How he wished for some good snail stew!

"Zzzzzzz," Ms. Mumfrey said. She was asleep.

"Psst!" Fenny said. "I want to go home."

"Me too," Crag said.

The two swamp monsters tiptoed from the room. They ran and ran and they didn't stop until they were home.

"I'm glad we saw children," Fenny said. "And tried noodles and ice cream."

"But I'm glad to be home," Crag said.

"I like swamp life better," Fenny agreed.

Mrs. Monster was baking mud pie for dessert.

"If we are real good, do we get mud pie?" Crag asked.

Mrs. Monster hugged them both. "I don't see why not! And if you are *extra* good, I'll read a story too."

"Yeah," Crag said. "A scary one!"

"About children!" Fenny agreed.

# SWAMP TIMES

Crag and Fenny may want to tell everyone about the day they played Children. Write a newspaper story that could appear in their local paper. Call your story "What Children Are Really Like." Draw a picture to go with your news story. As you write your story, remember that Crag and Fenny did not really understand everything they saw and did.

# Poems
# to Make
# You Laugh

# What Did?

What did the carrot say to the wheat?

"'Lettuce' rest, I'm feeling 'beet.'"

What did the paper say to the pen?

"I feel quite all 'write,' my friend."

What did the teapot say to the chalk?

Nothing, you silly . . . teapots can't talk!

Shel Silverstein

# The Folk Who Live in Backward Town

The folk who live in Backward Town

Are inside out and upside down.

They wear their hats inside their heads

And go to sleep beneath their beds.

They only eat the apple peeling

And take their walks across the ceiling.

Mary Ann Hoberman

# A Puppy

A puppy whose hair was so flowing
There really was no means of knowing
Which end was his head,
Once stopped me and said,
"Please, sir, am I coming or going?"

Oliver Herford

# Eletelephony

Once there was an elephant,
Who tried to use the telephant—
No! No! I mean an elephone
Who tried to use the telephone—
(Dear me I am not certain quite
That even now I've got it right.)

Howe'er it was he got his trunk
Entangled in the telephunk;
The more he tried to get it free,
The louder buzzed the telephee—
(I fear I'd better drop the song
Of elephop and telephong!)

Laura E. Richards

110

# Bananananananananana

I thought I'd win the spelling bee
   And get right to the top,
But I started to spell "banana,"
   And I didn't know when to stop.

William Cole

# At the Beach

—Johnny, Johnny, let go of that crab!
You have only ten fingers, you know:
If you hold it that way, it is certain to grab
At least one or two of them.  Please, let go!

—Thank you, Daddy, for teaching not scolding,
But there's one thing I think you should know:
I believe it's the crab that is doing the holding—
I let go—OUCH!—ten minutes ago!

John Ciardi

# There Was a Sad Pig with a Tail

There was a sad pig with a tail
Not curly, but straight as a nail.
So he ate simply oodles
Of pretzels and noodles,
Which put a fine twist to his tail.

Arnold Lobel

# Bursting

We've laughed until my cheeks are tight.
We've laughed until my stomach's sore.
If we could only stop we might
Remember what we're laughing for.

Dorothy Aldis

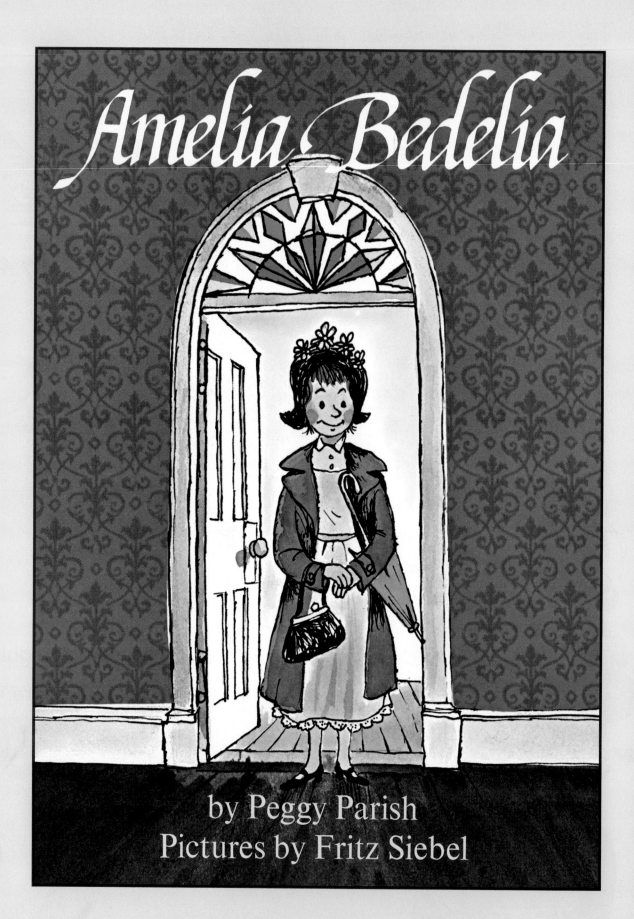

# Amelia Bedelia

by Peggy Parish
Pictures by Fritz Siebel

"Oh, Amelia Bedelia, your first day of work. And I can't be here. But I made a list for you. You do just what the list says," said Mrs. Rogers. Mrs. Rogers got into the car with Mr. Rogers. They drove away.

"My, what nice folks. I'm going to like working here," said Amelia Bedelia.

Amelia Bedelia went inside. "Such a grand house. These must be rich folks. But I must get to work. Here I stand just looking. And me with a whole list of things to do."

Amelia Bedelia stood there a minute longer. "I think I'll make a surprise for them. I'll make a lemon-meringue pie. I do make good pies."

So Amelia Bedelia went into the kitchen. She put a little of this and a pinch of that into a bowl. She mixed and she rolled. Soon her pie was ready to go into the oven.

"There," said Amelia Bedelia. "That's done. Now let's see what this list says."

Amelia Bedelia read,

*Change the towels in the green bathroom.*

Amelia Bedelia found the green bathroom.

"Those towels are very nice. Why change them?" she thought. Then Amelia Bedelia remembered what Mrs. Rogers had said. She must do just what the list told her.

"Well, all right," said Amelia Bedelia.

Amelia Bedelia got some scissors. She snipped a little here and a little there. And she changed those towels.

"There," said Amelia Bedelia. She looked at her list again.

## Dust the furniture.

"Did you ever hear tell of such a silly thing? At my house we undust the furniture. But to each his own way."

Amelia Bedelia took one last look at the bathroom. She saw a big box with the words *Dusting Powder* on it.

"Well, look at that. A special powder to dust with!" exclaimed Amelia Bedelia.

So Amelia Bedelia dusted the furniture.

"That should be dusty enough. My, how nice it smells."

# Draw the drapes when the sun comes in.

read Amelia Bedelia. She looked up. The sun was coming in. Amelia Bedelia looked at the list again.

"Draw the drapes? That's what it says. I'm not much of a hand at drawing, but I'll try."

So Amelia Bedelia sat right down and she drew those drapes. Amelia Bedelia marked off about the drapes.

"Now what?"

*Put the lights out when you finish in the living room.*

Amelia Bedelia thought about this a minute. She switched off the lights. Then she carefully unscrewed each bulb. And Amelia Bedelia put the lights out.

"So those things need to be aired out, too. Just like pillows and babies. Oh, I do have a lot to learn."

"My pie!" exclaimed Amelia Bedelia. She hurried to the kitchen.

"Just right," she said. She took the pie out of the oven and put it on the table to cool. Then she looked at the list.

Measure two cups of rice.

"That's next," said Amelia Bedelia. Amelia Bedelia found two cups. She filled them with rice. And Amelia Bedelia measured that rice.

Amelia Bedelia laughed. "These folks do want me to do funny things." Then she poured the rice back into the container.

The meat market will deliver
a steak, and a chicken.

Please trim the fat before you
put the steak in the icebox.

And please dress the chicken.

When the meat arrived, Amelia
Bedelia opened the bag. She
looked at the steak for a long time.

"Yes," she said. "That will do
nicely."

Amelia Bedelia got some lace
and bits of ribbon. And Amelia
Bedelia trimmed that fat before she
put the steak in the icebox.

"Now I must dress the chicken. I
wonder if she wants a he chicken or
a she chicken?" said Amelia Bedelia.

Amelia Bedelia went right to
work. Soon the chicken was finished.

Amelia Bedelia heard the
door open.

"The folks are back," she said.
She rushed out to meet them.

"Amelia Bedelia, why are all the light bulbs outside?" asked Mr. Rogers.

"The list just said to put the lights out," said Amelia Bedelia. "It didn't say to bring them back in. Oh, I do hope they didn't get aired too long."

"Amelia Bedelia, the sun will fade the furniture. I asked you to draw the drapes," said Mrs. Rogers.

"I did! I did! See," said Amelia Bedelia. She held up her picture.

Then Mrs. Rogers saw the furniture. "The furniture!" she cried.

"Did I dust it well enough?" asked Amelia Bedelia. "That's such nice dusting powder."

Mr. Rogers went to wash his hands. "I say," he called. "These are very unusual towels."

Mrs. Rogers dashed into the bathroom. "Oh, my best towels," she said.

"Didn't I change them enough?" asked Amelia Bedelia.

Mrs. Rogers went to the kitchen. "I'll cook the dinner. Where is the rice I asked you to measure?"

"I put it back in the container. But I remember — it measured four and a half inches," said Amelia Bedelia.

"Was the meat delivered?" asked Mrs. Rogers.

"Yes," said Amelia Bedelia. "I trimmed the fat just like you said. It does look nice."

Mrs. Rogers rushed to the icebox. She opened it.

"Lace! Ribbons! Oh, dear!" said Mrs. Rogers.

"The chicken — you dressed the chicken?" asked Mrs. Rogers.

"Yes, and I found the nicest box to put him in," said Amelia Bedelia.

"Box!" exclaimed Mrs. Rogers.

Mrs. Rogers hurried over to the box. She lifted the lid. There lay the chicken. And he was just as dressed as he could be.

    Mrs. Rogers was angry. She was very angry. She opened her mouth. Mrs. Rogers meant to tell Amelia Bedelia she was fired. But before she could get the words out, Mr. Rogers put something in her mouth. It was so good Mrs. Rogers forgot about being angry.

    "Lemon-meringue pie!" she exclaimed.

    "I made it to surprise you," said Amelia Bedelia happily. So right then and there Mr. and Mrs. Rogers decided that Amelia Bedelia must stay. And so she did.

Mrs. Rogers learned to say undust the furniture, unlight the lights, close the drapes, and things like that. Mr. Rogers didn't care if Amelia Bedelia trimmed all of his steaks with lace.

All he cared about was having her there to make lemon-meringue pie.

TOSS THE SALAD
ICE THE CAKE
MAKE THE BED
BEAT THE EGGS
STAMP THE LETTER

# DON'T FORGET TO...

In the story, Mrs. Rogers left a list of jobs for Amelia to do, and Amelia got everything mixed up. Imagine that Mrs. Rogers left the list at the top of this page for Amelia.

With a partner, act out each job on the list. Take turns acting out the way Mrs. Rogers wants the job done and the way Amelia Bedelia might really do the job.

# About the Authors

## Keiko Kasza

Keiko Kasza started writing books in Japan, where she was born. While living there, she wrote and illustrated several children's books in Japanese. Kasza now lives in the United States with her family. *The Wolf's Chicken Stew* is the first book she has published here.

## Mary Blount Christian

Mary Blount Christian has always loved to read. When she was young, she would roller-skate two miles to the library. She wanted to read every book there. "I started with the A's and worked my way around the shelves," she says. Now that Christian is grown up, she still likes to read funny stories and even write them. If you'd like to read more about Crag and Fenny, read *Go West, Swamp Monsters*. In this book, Crag and Fenny find many adventures in their search for a new home.

## Peggy Parish

When Peggy Parish was a child, she enjoyed playing with other children. But she also enjoyed being alone because she could read as many books as she wanted. She loved books so much that when she grew up she wrote her own books. *Amelia Bedelia* was her first book

about Amelia the maid who gets into trouble by doing exactly what she is asked to do. Some other books about Amelia Bedelia's mixed-up adventures are *Amelia Bedelia Goes Camping; Play Ball, Amelia Bedelia;* and *Amelia Bedelia's Family Album*.

# A Laugh From Cover To Cover

*Monkey-Monkey's Trick*
by Patricia McKissack

Monkey-Monkey needs to build a new home.  A pot of stew and a beautiful creature may be able to help him.

*Four on the Shore*
by Edward Marshall

See who gets the last laugh when Lolly and her friends try to frighten Willie with their scary stories.

## The Stupids Step Out
by Harry Allard

Here are the Stupids — a family who walk on their hands and eat mashed potato sundaes!

## Henry Goes West
by Robert Quackenbush

Lots of silly things happen when Henry goes out West to visit his friend Clara.

131

- What is bigger than a million earths all put together?

- What is a stegosaurus (steg-uh-SAW-russ)?

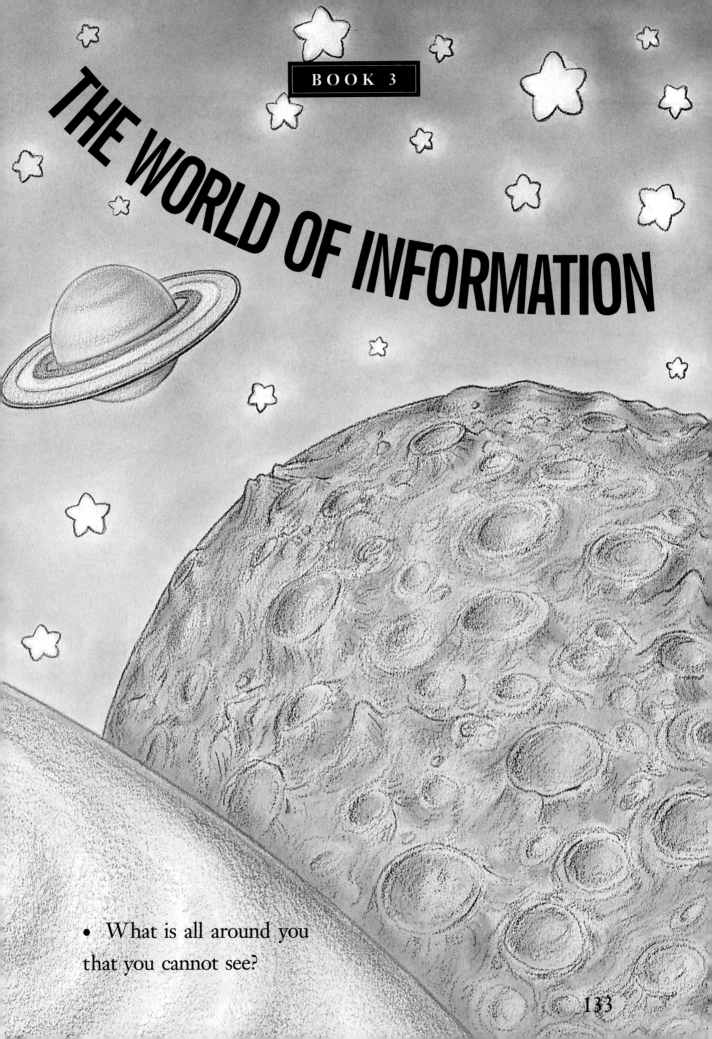

# BOOK 3

# THE WORLD OF INFORMATION

- What is all around you
  that you cannot see?

133

Nonfiction books tell about real people, real animals, and real places. They answer questions, explain how things work, and tell about things that actually happened.

You will find the answers to the questions on pages 132 and 133 in the nonfiction selections in this book. For other questions you might have, your library is full of nonfiction books on every subject you can imagine.

Welcome to the World of Information.

# CONTENTS

*Do You Know About Stars?*    136
written by Mae Blacker Freeman
with illustrations by Fred Lynch

*Dinosaur Time*    156
written by Peggy Parish
with illustrations by Arnold Lobel

*Air Is All Around You*    180
written by Franklyn M. Branley
with illustrations by Holly Keller

# Do You Know About Stars?

by Mae Blacker Freeman

illustrated by Fred Lynch

Look up at the sky at night. You can see many stars. They shine and twinkle.
There are
millions
of millions
of millions
of millions
of stars in the sky. There are so many stars in the sky — more than you could ever count.

When you look at a star, it seems so tiny. All things look tiny when they are far away from you. Even big things look tiny if they are far away.

**An airplane is very big.** It can hold many people. But . . . look at an airplane when it is high in the sky. Then it does not look big at all. It looks like a toy. The airplane looks tiny because it is far away.

Stars look tiny, too, because they are far away. But stars are really big, big, big. Almost every star is much bigger than the whole earth.

All stars are far, far away.  But there is one star that is not as far away as the others.

It is a star that you know very well because you see it shine in the daytime.  Do you know which star it is?

It is the sun. . . . The sun is a star! The sun is big and round and very, very bright. The sun does not look tiny like the other stars. That is because the other stars are much farther away than the sun. The sun is bigger than a million earths all put together.

Can you ride
an airplane to a
star? No. There is no
air out in space. A plane
can fly only where there is air.
But a rocket can go to the sun.
It takes many months to get there. A
rocket could even go on, to the next star.
But nobody could ride in that rocket. The
trip would take too long. The trip would take
thousands of years.

144

Suppose you could get near the sun or near any other star. What would it look like? The sun would look like a huge ball of clouds. But the clouds are not like the fluffy white ones that you see in a blue sky. And they are not like the dark gray clouds that you see on a rainy day.

A star is made of clouds that are different. They are very, very bright and very, very hot. The clouds of a star are orange and yellow and white. They tumble and toss and swoop and swirl. Huge red flares shoot out and loop back again.

148

Even if you could
get near the sun or any
other star, you could not look
at it.  It is much too bright.  You must
never look right at the sun, even from here
on earth.  It would harm your eyes.
How hot is a star?  Think of some things
that are hot.  Think of a hot summer day . . .
or hot sand on the beach. Think of

# FIRE!

Are any of these things
as hot as a star?

No!  A star is much, much hotter.  A star is hotter than anything you can think of.

But YOU cannot feel how hot a star is. YOU cannot tell that a star is a ball of hot clouds that tumble and toss and swoop and swirl.  The stars are too far away.

For YOU, stars are bright dots that twinkle in the dark sky. Look up at the sky tonight and see.

# Now I Know About Stars

On a sheet of paper, draw a large star. On each of the five points of the star, write a fact that you have learned about the stars. Follow the steps below to help you draw your star.

## How to draw a star in five easy steps

## Mae Blacker Freeman

Mae Blacker Freeman writes informational books on many different subjects. She is a photographer as well as a writer. One book that she wrote about ballet included pictures of her daughter as the ballet dancer.

Another book by Mae Blacker Freeman that is full of interesting facts is *Do You Know About Water?*

# Stars in the Sea

At night there are many stars in the sky. Did you know that there are animals shaped like stars? They are called sea stars, or **starfish.**

Starfish live in the ocean. But they are not true fish. They grow in many sizes, shapes, and colors.

Most starfish have five arms. Some have even more! If a starfish breaks off an arm, it can grow a new one. This makes starfish very different from other animals.

# Dinosaur Time

*by Peggy Parish*

*with illustrations by Arnold Lobel*

Long, long ago the world was different.
More land was under water. It was warm all
the time. And dinosaurs were everywhere. . . .
There were big dinosaurs. There were
small ones. There were fast dinosaurs, and
slow ones. Some dinosaurs ate meat. Some
ate plants.

# Stegosaurus

## STEGOSAURUS

This is how you say it —
steg-uh-SAW-russ

This dinosaur had plates on its back.
They were made of bone.  It had sharp points
on its tail.  It ate plants.  Its name is
Stegosaurus.


## ANKYLOSAURUS

This is how you say it —
ank-eye-loh-SAW-russ

This dinosaur had a shell like a turtle.  Its
tail was like a club.  Not many animals could
hurt it.  Its name is Ankylosaurus.


## COMPSOGNATHUS

This is how you say it —
comp-sog-NAYTH-uss

This dinosaur was small.  It was as big as
a cat.  But it could run fast.  It could catch
other animals and eat them.  Its name is
Compsognathus.

Ankylosaurus

# Compsognathus

## BRONTOSAURUS

This is how you say it —
bron-tuh-SAW-russ

This dinosaur was a giant.  But its mouth was tiny.  It ate plants.  It ate, and ate, and ate to fill up its big body.  Its name is Brontosaurus.

## PENTACERATOPS

This is how you say it —
pen-tuh-SARE-ah-tops

This dinosaur had five horns. They were all on its face. Its name is Pentaceratops. This name is just right. It means "five-horns-on-the-face."

## DIPLODOCUS

This is how you say it —
dip-LAH-duh-cuss

This dinosaur was long.  But most of it was neck and tail.  Its teeth were short and dull.  It ate plants.  Its name is Diplodocus.

# Teratosaurus

## TERATOSAURUS

This is how you say it —
tare-at-oh-SAW-russ

This dinosaur walked on its back legs.  It
had big claws, and sharp teeth.  It ate meat.
Its name is Teratosaurus.

## ANATOSAURUS

This is how you say it —
an-at-oh-SAW-russ

This dinosaur is called a "duckbill."  It
had a beak like a duck.  Its beak had no teeth.
But its mouth did.  There were hundreds of
teeth in it!  Sometimes a tooth broke.  But
that did not matter.  It could grow a new one.
Its name is Anatosaurus.

## ORNITHOMIMUS

This is how you say it —
or-nith-oh-MY-muss

This dinosaur had a beak, too.  But it had
no teeth.  It ate small animals and insects.
Maybe it ate fruits and dinosaur eggs, too.
But it had no teeth.  How did it eat?  A bird
eats.  It has no teeth.  Maybe it ate like a
bird.  Its name is Ornithomimus.

# Anatosaurus

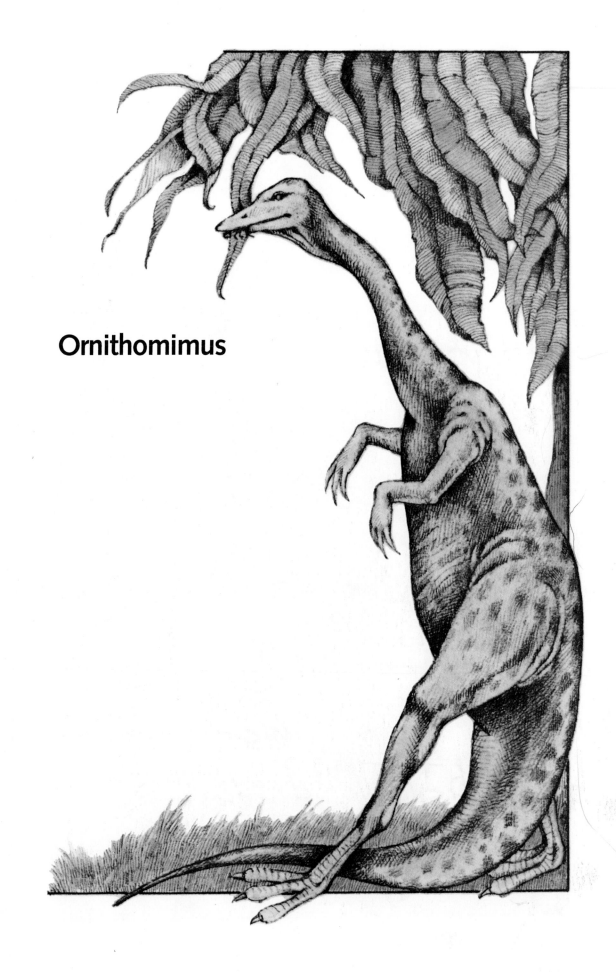

**Ornithomimus**

## BRACHIOSAURUS

This is how you say it —
brack-ee-oh-SAW-russ

This dinosaur was fat. It was too fat to run from enemies. That is why it stayed in the water. It was safe there, and food was close by. It ate plants. Its name is Brachiosaurus.

# TYRANNOSAURUS

This is how you say it —
tih-ran-uh-SAW-russ

This dinosaur was the biggest meat-eater. Its jaws were huge. Its teeth were six inches long. It ate other dinosaurs. Its name is Tyrannosaurus.

Dinosaurs lived everywhere for a long time. Then they died. Nobody knows why. But once it was their world. It was dinosaur time.

175

## DINOSAUR FACTS

In this story you learned about different kinds of dinosaurs. Which kind of dinosaur did you think was the most interesting? Discuss with a partner the dinosaur you liked best. Then tell your partner some facts about that dinosaur.

**Peggy Parish**

Peggy Parish was a third grade teacher before she began writing books for children. You may have already read *Amelia Bedelia,* one of her funniest books.

Another nonfiction book by this author is *Beginning Mobiles.* In this book you can learn how to make easy holiday decorations.

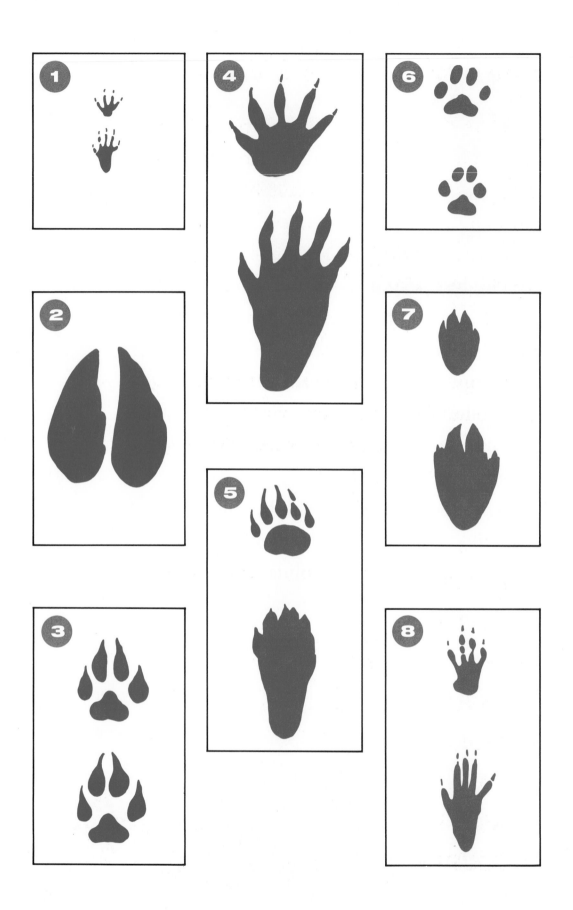

# Animal Tracks

Have you ever made a footprint in the snow or sand? Dinosaurs left large footprints in the earth. Footprints made by animals are called **tracks**.

On page 178 there are some animal tracks you might find in a park or in a forest. At the bottom of this page, you can learn which animals made these tracks.

If you go looking for animal tracks, study the ground carefully. Now you might be able to recognize animal tracks when you see them.

1 MOUSE
2 DEER
3 DOG
4 RACCOON
5 SKUNK
6 CAT
7 RABBIT
8 SQUIRREL

# Air Is All

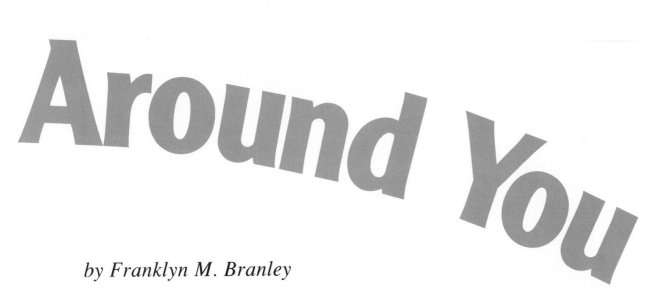

# Around You

*by Franklyn M. Branley*

*with illustrations by Holly Keller*

Air is all around you. There is air down in a deep valley. There is air around a high mountain. Wherever you go, there is air.

Cars and houses are filled with it. So are barns, sheds, doghouses and birdhouses.

Cups are full of it. So are bowls, pots and glasses that we drink out of.

That's hard to believe because you can't see the air, or smell it. You can't feel it either, except when it's moving. Or when you spin around.

You can't see the air in a glass, but you can prove it is there.  Try this experiment.

Run a lot of water into the sink.  Or put water in a big bowl.  Color the water with a little food coloring. Not much, just enough to color it a little bit.

Stuff a paper napkin into the bottom of a glass. Turn the glass upside down.  If the napkin falls out, stuff it in tighter.

Keep the glass upside down.  Make sure it is straight up and down.  Do not tip it.  Push it all the way under the water.  Or as far under as you can.

Lift the glass out of the water. Turn it right side up and take out the paper napkin. It is dry. The water did not touch it. The paper was under the water. But it did not get wet. Let's see why.

Once again put the napkin in the glass. Turn the glass upside down, and push it under the water.

Look at the glass through the water. The water does not go into it.

It can't go in because there is air in the glass. But you can make the water go in.

Tip the glass a little bit. A bubble of air goes out and up.

When the air goes out, there is empty space in the glass. Water goes in.

You can see it. The coloring you added to the water helps you see it. Bubbles go out, and water goes in.

Keep tipping the glass until all the air goes out. Now it is full of water and the napkin is soaking wet.

When the glass was full of air, there was no room for water. When the air went out, the water went in.

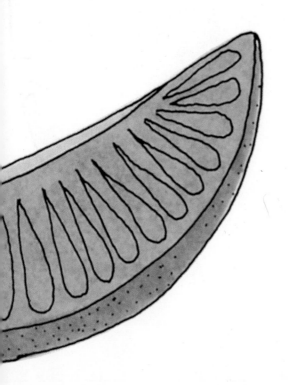

Air is all around you, and it is all around the earth.  Air covers the earth like peel covers an orange.

The air weighs a lot — 5 quadrillion tons.  That's 5,000,000,000,000,000 tons.  That's hard to believe, but it's true.

The air in the room where you are weighs more than you think.  In an average room, the air weighs seventy-five pounds or so.  If the room is big, the air in it weighs more.  If it is small, the air weighs less.  We don't feel it because the air is spread all around us.

Airplanes and balloons fly in the air. But spaceships don't. Rockets push them higher than the air. Spaceships fly above the air that is all around the earth.

Spaceships must take air with them. They have enough to keep the astronauts alive. When they go out of the ship, astronauts carry tanks of air on their backs. They need air to stay alive. And so do you and I.

Lucky for us, air is everywhere. Wherever we go on earth, there is air. Air is even in water. That's lucky for fish. The air is dissolved in the water. You can't see the air. But you can prove that it is there.

Fill a glass with water. Set the glass aside and leave it for an hour.

After an hour you will see little bubbles on the inside of the glass. They are tiny bubbles of air. The air came out of the water.

Fish use the air that is dissolved in water. They have gills that help them do this. Air keeps them alive.

We can't breathe air that is dissolved in water. So when we stay under water a long time, we have to take air with us. Divers take air in tanks strapped to their backs.

Air keeps us alive.

Wherever we go on earth — north, south, east or west, high on a mountain or deep in a valley — there is air.

Air is all around us.

# SHARE WHAT YOU KNOW

The selection you just read tells you lots of facts about air. Do you know facts about another subject such as dogs, airplanes, or foods? Pick a subject that you know a lot about. Write five sentences about that subject, and draw a picture to go along with it. Then trade your information with a friend and share what you know.

WORLD
of
FACTS

## Franklyn M. Branley

Franklyn M. Branley was a teacher and decided to write books for children about science because he couldn't find many books that his students could read. He enjoys it so much that he has written over sixty books on all kinds of topics.

Here are two you might enjoy reading.

*What Makes Day and Night* Why don't we feel the earth turning? How long is night on the moon? This book tells you all the facts.

*Big Tracks, Little Tracks* Sometimes you see footprints in the sand or the snow. The clues to tell what kind of animal made them are in this book.

# THE WORLD OF BOOKS

*The Biggest, Smallest, Fastest, Tallest Things You've Ever Heard Of*
by Robert Lopshire

What is the smallest horse in the world? What town has the longest name? The answers to these questions and many more are in this amazing nonfiction book.

*Keep Looking!* by Millicent Selsam and Joyce Hunt

The farmhouse and yard look empty on a snowy day. But if you look at and read this book closely, you will see the animals hiding in their homes.

*Zoo* by Gail Gibbons

Find out who takes care of the elephant with a stomachache. Who feeds the animals each day?

*A Picture Book of George Washington* by David A. Adler

Find out about the farmer who became the first president of the United States.

*How A Book Is Made* by Aliki

This book by Aliki takes you through all the steps of how a book is made.

# Glossary

This glossary can help you find out the meanings of some of the words in this book. The meanings given are the meanings of the words as the words are used in the book. Sometimes a second meaning is also given.

**amazing** Surprising: *That is an **amazing** ending to the story.*

**astronaut** A person who is trained to ride in a spacecraft. An astronaut checks the controls of a spacecraft before it goes into space.

**beak** The hard, pointed mouth, or bill, of a bird: *The duckbill dinosaur had a wide, flat **beak**.*

beak

**bother** To worry or trouble: *My little brother always comes to **bother** me when I am doing my homework.*

**brag** To talk about yourself or things you have done: *Everyone knows Mark got an "A" on the test because he keeps **bragging** about it.*

**claw** A sharp nail on the toe of an animal or bird: *Some birds use their **claws** to hold onto tree branches.*

*claw*

**club** A long, heavy stick used as a weapon. Some dinosaurs had tails shaped like clubs and used them to fight off other dinosaurs.

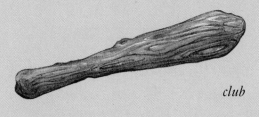

*club*

**collection** A group of things that a person gathers and keeps together as a hobby: *Nan has stamps from all over the world in her stamp **collection**.*

**craving** A strong wish or longing: *Lila has a **craving** for chicken.*

**delicious** Tasting or smelling very good: *The meal was **delicious**.*

**deliver** To bring or carry: *The flower shop will **deliver** the flowers to our house.*

**dissolve** To mix completely with a liquid: *After the powder was **dissolved** in the water, the water turned red.*

**draw 1.** To make a picture with a pencil or crayons: *Jeanne likes to **draw** pictures of trees.* **2.** To pull together to close. To draw the curtains means to close them.

**dull** Not having a sharp edge or point: *The pencil was so **dull** that it was hard to write with it.*

**dust** To remove dirt by wiping or brushing: ***Dust** the shelves before you put the books back on them.*

**enemy** One who hurts or wants to hurt another: *The cat is an **enemy** of the mouse.*

**exclaim** To speak suddenly and loudly, as if surprised: *"Look what I found!" Jill **exclaimed**.*

**experiment** A test used to find out or prove something: *The **experiment** proved that air is everywhere.*

**fasten** To attach one thing to another: *Carol used tape to **fasten** the string to the kite.*

**fire** To let go or send away from a job: *Bob was **fired** from his job because he didn't work very hard.*

**flare** A sudden burst of light. Stars shoot off huge red flares.

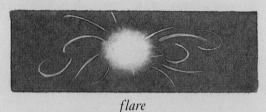

*flare*

**food coloring** A liquid used to change the color of food: *Jim used **food coloring** to make the cake frosting pink.*

**jaws** The pair of bones in the mouth that hold the teeth.

*jaws*

**jerk** To move suddenly and sharply: *When my dog pulled on his leash, the leash **jerked** in my hand.*

**kelp** A brown plant that lives in the sea. Kelp is a type of seaweed.

**kite** A light wooden frame covered with cloth, paper, or plastic: *We are going to fly our **kite** on the next windy day.*

**knob** A round dial or handle used to turn a TV or radio on and off.

*knob*

**measure** To find the size or amount of something: *Dad will **measure** the floor to be sure to buy a rug that is the right size.*

**meringue** A topping for pies, made of beaten egg whites: *Meg baked a lemon **meringue** pie.*

**metal** A material, such as iron or copper, that is hard and shiny. Swing sets are usually made of metal.

**million** A very large number. A million is a larger number than a thousand: *There are **millions** of stars in the sky.*

**monster** An imaginary creature that is strange and sometimes frightening: *Danny wasn't scared of the **monsters** in the story because he knew they weren't real.*

**mope** To be sad and silent: *When it rained and she couldn't go camping, Beth **moped** around the house.*

**peek** To look at quickly or secretly: *The children **peeked** through the bushes where they were hiding.*

**perfect** Very good in every way: *A sunny day is **perfect** for going to the beach.*

**perform** To sing, dance, or do something else in front of a group of people: *All the people in our neighborhood came to see us* **perform** *our play.*

**practice** Something done over and over in order to become good at it: *It takes a lot of* **practice** *to play the piano well.*

**prey** An animal hunted by another animal for food: *Chickens are the* **prey** *of wolves.*

**principal** The person in charge of a school: *The* **principal** *met all the new students on the first day of school.*

**promise** To say that you will do something: *I* **promised** *my mother that I would clean my room today.*

**prove** To show that something is true: *The experiment* **proved** *that there is air in an empty glass.*

**rocket** A powerful aircraft that burns fuel very fast.

*rocket*

**rumble** To make a deep, long, rolling sound, like thunder: *If you are very hungry, your stomach might* **rumble**.

**scrumptious** Very tasty and delicious: *The baker made* **scrumptious** *cookies and cakes that everyone loved.*

**secret** Something known only to one person or a small group: *The two friends have* **secrets** *that they don't tell anyone.*

**seriously** In a way that is not fooling or joking: *Pete wondered what was wrong when his father spoke so seriously*.

**sharp** Pointed or having a thin edge that cuts: *The knife is not sharp enough to cut the meat*.

**sigh** To let out a long, deep breathing sound because one is sad or tired: *Juan sighed unhappily when I told him I was moving away*.

**snip** To cut with short, quick movements: *Sally snipped the cloth with her scissors*.

snip

**snort** To make a loud sound by forcing air through the nose: *The horse snorted loudly when we came near it*.

**space** The area in which the sun, stars, and planets are found.

**stew** A thick soup that is cooked very slowly. A chicken stew might be made of chicken, vegetables, and water.

stew

**straighten out** To help someone behave or act better. If you straighten out someone, it means you talk to that person and explain what he or she is doing wrong.

**swamp** A flat area of muddy land that is covered with water. Many animals, such as alligators and birds, live in a swamp.

swamp

**swirl** To spin or move in circles very quickly: *The snowflakes swirled around in the strong wind.*

**swoop** To fly or move in a sudden sweeping way: *A large bird swooped down from the sky.*

## T

**tail 1.** The part of an animal's body that is farthest to the rear: *When dogs are happy, they wag their tails.* **2.** The string or cloth that hangs from the bottom of a kite to help the kite fly straight.

**tease** To bother someone by making fun of him or her: *My uncle used to tease me about being taller than all my cousins.*

**terrible** Very bad: *The movie was so terrible that we all left before it was over.*

**terrific** Very good: *It was a terrific party.*

**thousand** A large number. A thousand is a larger number than a hundred.

**tip** To slant something or make one side higher than the other: *Make sure the glass is straight up and down. Do not tip it.*

**trim 1.** To make neat or even by cutting. To trim the fat from the meat means to cut the fat away. **2.** To make fancy or beautiful: *Lisa trimmed the box with ribbons and bows.*

*trim*

**twinkle** To shine with quick flashes of light: *Stars twinkle in the sky at night.*

## U

**unscrew** To remove by twisting: *My mother unscrewed the old light bulb and put in a new one.*

**unusual** Not happening often or all the time: *It is **unusual** for John to walk to school because most days his father drives him.*

**usually** Happening very often or all the time: *Some mornings Brian has eggs, but he **usually** has cereal for breakfast.*

**wait** To stay in a place until something happens: *Marie said she would call this morning, so we **waited** by the telephone.*

**weigh** To measure how heavy something is: *You can **weigh** your dog on this scale.*

**zipper** A fastener that is made up of two rows of metal or plastic teeth and a tab that locks them together. Many jackets and coats open and close with zippers.

*zipper*

# Acknowledgments

For each of the selections listed below, grateful acknowledgment is made for permission to excerpt and/or reprint original or copyrighted material, as follows:

**Major Selections**

*Air Is All Around You*, by Franklyn M. Branley, illustrated by Holly Keller. Text copyright © 1962, 1986 by Franklyn M. Branley. Illustrations copyright © 1986 by Holly Keller. Reprinted by permission of Harper & Row, Publishers, Inc.

*Amelia Bedelia*, by Peggy Parish, illustrated by Fritz Siebel. Text copyright © 1963 by Margaret Parish. Illustrations copyright © 1963 by Fritz Siebel. Reprinted by permission of Harper & Row, Publishers, Inc.

*Dinosaur Time*, by Peggy Parish. Text copyright © 1974 by Margaret Parish. Illustrations copyright © 1974 by Arnold Lobel. Reprinted by permission of Harper & Row, Publishers, Inc. and Heinemann Children's Books.

*Do You Know About Stars?* by Mae Blacker Freeman. Copyright © 1970 by Mae Blacker Freeman. Reprinted by permission of Random House, Inc.

"Gloria Who Might Be My Best Friend," from *The Stories Julian Tells*, by Ann Cameron. Copyright © 1981 by Ann Cameron. Reprinted by permission of Random House Inc., and Victor Gollancz Ltd.

*Ira Says Goodbye*, by Bernard Waber. Copyright © 1988 by Bernard Waber. Reprinted by permission of Houghton Mifflin Company and Curtis Brown, Ltd.

*Lizzie and Harold*, by Elizabeth Winthrop, illustrated by Martha Weston. Copyright © 1986 by Elizabeth Winthrop. Illustrations copyright © 1986 by Martha Weston. Reprinted by permission of Lothrop, Lee and Shepard Books, a division of William Morrow and Co.

*Swamp Monsters*, by Mary Blount Christian, pictures by Marc Brown. Text copyright © 1983 by Mary Blount Christian. Pictures copyright © 1983 by Marc Brown. Reprinted by permission of the publisher, Dial Books for Young Readers.

*The Wolf's Chicken Stew*, by Keiko Kasza. Copyright © 1987 by Keiko Kasza. Reprinted by permission of G.P. Putnam's Sons and Geoffrey Bles, Ltd.

**Poetry**

"At the Beach," by John Ciardi, from *Doodle Soup*. Copyright © 1985 by Myra J. Ciardi. Reprinted by permission of Houghton Mifflin Company.

"Banananananananana," by William Cole. Copyright © 1977 by William Cole. Reprinted by permission of the author.

"Bursting," by Dorothy Aldis, from *All Together*. Copyright 1952 by Dorothy Aldis, copyright © renewed 1980 by Roy E. Porter. Reprinted by permission of G.P. Putnam's Sons.

"Eletelephony," by Laura E. Richards, from *Tirra Lirra: Rhymes Old and New*. Copyright 1930, 1932 by Laura E. Richards. Copyright © renewed 1960 by Hamilton Richards. Reprinted by permission of Little, Brown and Company.

"The Folk Who Live in Backward Town," in *Hello and Good-By*, by Mary Ann Hoberman. Copyright © 1959 by Mary Ann Hoberman, renewed 1987. Reprinted by permission of the Gina Maccoby Literary Agency.

"A puppy whose hair was so flowing," by Oliver Herford. Copyright 1912 The Century Co.

"Since Hanna Moved Away," by Judith Viorst, from *If I Were in Charge of the World and Other Worries*. Copyright © 1981 by Judith Viorst. Reprinted by permission of Atheneum Publishers, an imprint of Macmillan Publishing Company, and Lescher and Lescher.

"There was a sad pig with a tail," by Arnold Lobel. Copyright © 1983 by Arnold Lobel. Reprinted from *The Book of Pigericks* by permission of Harper & Row, Publishers, Inc., and Jonathan Cape Ltd.

"Two Friends," by Nikki Giovanni, from *Spin a Soft Black Song*. Copyright © 1971, 1985 by Nikki Giovanni. Reprinted by permission of Farrar, Straus and Giroux.

"What Did?" by Shel Silverstein, from *A Light in the Attic*. Copyright © 1981 by Evil Eye Music, Inc. Reprinted by permission of Harper & Row, Publishers, Inc., and Jonathan Cape Ltd.

"What Johnny Told Me," by John Ciardi, from *Fast and Slow*. Copyright © 1975 by John Ciardi. Reprinted by permission of Houghton Mifflin Company.

**Quotations from Authors/Illustrators**

Mary Blount Christian, page 129, from *Something About the Author*, vol. 9. Copyright © 1976 by Gale Research Inc. Reprinted by permission of the publisher.

**Theme Books**

The Theme Books shown on Extended Reading pages are available from Houghton Mifflin Company and are reprinted with permission from various publishers. Jacket artists for these books are listed below.

*The Biggest, Smallest, Fastest, Tallest Things You've Ever Heard Of*, by Robert Lopshire. Jacket art by Robert Lopshire, copyright © 1980 by Robert Lopshire.

*Henry and Mudge*, by Cynthia Rylant. Jacket art by Suçie Stevenson, copyright © 1987 by Suçie Stevenson.

*Monkey-Monkey's Trick*, by Patricia McKissack. Jacket art by Paul Meisel, copyright © 1988 by Paul Meisel.

## Additional Recommended Reading

Houghton Mifflin Company wishes to thank the following publishers for permission to reproduce their book covers in Extended Reading lists:

Thomas Y. Crowell Company, imprint of Harper & Row Publishers, Inc.:
*How a Book Is Made*, by Aliki. Jacket art by Aliki, copyright © 1986 by Aliki Brandenberg; *Zoo*, by Gail Gibbons. Jacket art by Gail Gibbons, copyright © 1987 by Gail Gibbons.

Dial Books for Young Readers, a division of Penguin Books USA Inc.:
*Four on the Shore*, by Edward Marshall. Jacket art by James Marshall, copyright © 1985 by James Marshall. Published simultaneously in Canada by Fitzhenry & Whiteside Limited, Toronto.

Greenwillow Books, a division of William Morrow & Company, Inc.:
*Nice New Neighbors*, by Franz Brandenberg. Jacket art by Aliki, copyright © 1977 by Aliki Brandenberg.

Harper & Row Publishers, Inc.:
*Best Friends for Frances*, by Russell Hoban. Jacket art by Lillian Hoban, copyright © 1969 by Lillian Hoban. Published simultaneously in Canada by Fitzhenry & Whiteside Limited, Toronto; *The Hating Book*, by Charlotte Zolotow. Jacket art by Ben Shecter, copyright © 1969 by Ben Shecter. Published simultaneously in Canada by Fitzhenry & Whiteside Limited, Toronto.

Holiday House:
*A Picture Book of George Washington*, by David A. Adler. Jacket art by John and Alexandra Wallner, copyright © 1989 by John C. and Alexandra Wallner.

Houghton Mifflin Company:
*The Stupids Step Out*, by Harry Allard. Jacket art by James Marshall, copyright © 1974 by James Marshall.

Macmillan Publishing Company, Inc.:
*Keep Looking!*, by Millicent Selsam and Joyce Hunt. Jacket art by Normand Chartier, copyright © 1989 by Normand Chartier.

Giulio Maestro:
*Two Good Friends*, by Judy Delton. Jacket art by Giulio Maestro, copyright © 1974 by Giulio Maestro. Published simultaneously in Canada by General Publishing Company Limited.

Parents Magazine Press:
*Henry Goes West*, by Robert Quackenbush. Jacket art by Robert Quackenbush, copyright © 1982 by Robert Quackenbush.

## Credits

**Program design**   Carbone Smolan Associates

**Cover design**   Carbone Smolan Associates

**Design**   **8–75** TextArt;   **76–131** DeFrancis Studio; **132–197** Sheaff Design, Inc.

**Illustrations**   **8–11** Cat Bowman Smith;   **12–28** Martha Weston;   **29–31** Cat Bowman Smith;   **32–56** Bernard Waber;   **57** Cat Bowman Smith;   **58–70** Beth Peck;   **71–75** Cat Bowman Smith;   **76–79** Fred Schrier;   **80–90** Keiko Kasza;   **91** Fred Schrier;   **92–104** Marc Brown;   **105** Fred Schrier;   **106, 108–113** T.R. Garcia;   **107** Shel Silverstein;   **114–126** Fritz Siebel;   **127** Fred Schrier;   **130–131** Fred Schrier;   **132–135** Jim Connolly;   **136–151** Fred Lynch;   **152–153** Sheaff Design, Inc.;   **155** Jim Connolly;   **156–175** Arnold Lobel;   **176–178** Sheaff Design, Inc.;   **179** Jim Connolly;   **180–193** Holly Keller;   **194–195** Nancy Bernard;   **196–197** Jim Connolly;   **198, 199, 200** (top), **201, 203** (top right), **205** Meg Kelleher-Aubrey;   **200** (bottom), **203** (bottom left), **204** Jan Palmer

**Photography**   **72** (top left) Sarah Fletcher, (bottom right) courtesy of Bernard Waber;   **73** Das Anudas;   **128** courtesy of G.P. Putnam Sons;   **129** (bottom) Rick Foster;   **154** Gerald & Buff Corsi/Tom Stack & Associates;   **195** courtesy of Franklyn Branley;   **199** Royce Blair/The Stock Solution;   **202** NASA/Grant Heilman Photography, Inc.;   **203** Stephen G. Maka;   **Back cover** Van Williams

**End Matter**   production by Publicom, Inc.

207